The Fluid Chicano

poems by

Gabriel H. Sánchez

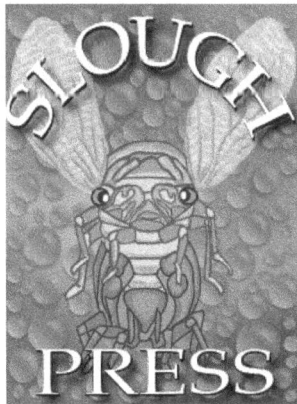

Slough Press   Kyle ~ Alamo

For orders and information:
Slough Press
334 Spring Dr.
Kyle, Texas 78640.
or
Slough Press
939 W. De Soto Ave.
Alamo, TX 78516

Cover Art by Malena Guitterez

Book Design by Christopher Carmona

Acknowledgements

"Chicano Renacido" first published in El Retorno: Our Serpent's Tongue, 2014

"Mi Amante Soledad" first published in riverSedge, 2014

"Aztec Love," "Barrio Flowers," "Song of Love" first published in Gallery 2004

ISBN: 978-0-941720-41-0

Library of Congress Control Number: 2015935674

Para 'Ma

Table of Contents

One: Fused by History

Valley of the Rio Grand...1
To Man...4
The Wall Is Coming Down..7
Moctezuma's Ghost..9
Free Isn't Freedom (For George W. Bush)..11
WMD Brain Freeze...14
Monkey See..16
War America...18
In Resonance to Serj Tankian's Comment on Civilization.................20
In Resonance, Part II: The Age of Reason.......................................22
After the End of Time...23
Waking the Dead...25
Brush Strokes (Of the End of the World)...26
Barrio Flowers..28
Bush *Era* Love..29
Search for the Burning Spear..30
Civilization Petrification...31
World of Conquest...32
I Am The Bridge..33
Flux...34

Two: An Internal Flux

Yearning...36
Father..37
Gone Dead..39
Landscapes of Eternity...40
Nothing Lasts Forever (The Cosmic Escape)....................................41
Lineage of Man...42
Obsession...43
Song of Love/Song of Death...45
I Wait..47
Butterfly in Amber...48
Lovers Born Anew..50
Aztec Love..51
My Paintings...53

The Freckles on Your Skin...54
In My Hands...55
Your Nectar...57
When Your Eyes Are Looking..58
Memories Soaked In Brine...59
To A-muse...you..60
To the Luteus Flower Blooming in my Window Sun.....................61
Wailing...62
Bouquet of Words...63

Three: Love, Too, Flows Through Fingers Like Water

Love in Rigor Mortis...65
Love in Rigor Mortis II--the Revisit..66
Winter Love..67
Soul's Budding...68
STD Romance...69
El Ave de Inspiración..70
My Inspiration (Translation of El Ave de mi Inspiracion) 71
Love is a Fiesta in the Night...72
Love on the Night Train...73
24 Hours...74
Mi Amante Soledad..75
My Lover Solitude (Translation of Mi Amante Soledad) 77
After All...78

Four: Fluidity of Identity

Change... 80
Palabras del Río...81
Terms of the River (Translation for Palabras del Rio) 82
Lost...83
Chicano Por Siempre..85
The Dead Chicano...86
Chicano Renacido..87
Chicano Reborn (Translation of Chicano Renacido) 88
South Texas Reservation...89
Paradise on Earth..91

Introduction

The concept of a Fluid Chicano is an ongoing investigation of the self in terms of my identity. Because I am part of a greater community, I hope my development will impact others around me. This book of poetry represents just one step in achieving the ultimate goal of fully expanding the concept in prose in the near future. For now, readers will see the concept represented in one way or another in several of the poems selected here. Identity is not a solid quality of a person, but a loosely understood idea, which requires a laundry list of criteria to check off in order to say that I am this or that; like saying I am American, or that others are something else not American. Our best bet is to maintain the idea present that we are first individuals capable of growth. That growth involves exposure to new ideas and things. That new ideas have the capacity to change our views and that change often brings up conflicts between the old self and the new. The old self is cemented and wishes to maintain; it is conservative. The new self is free, and wishes to remain open; it is fluid. If one thing resonates here to the reader I wish it would be this: that the most important aspect of being a Fluid Chicano is not the part of being a Chicano, but the Fluid one. Being a Chicano has its cap, it's ceiling. So, too, does simply being an American, Mexican, African, Russian, etc. have limits on the potential for growth. But being Fluid allows anyone regardless of race or nationality, the ability to transcend the self-imposed limitations, as well as the societal ones. The original identity of all men and women is the same: a blank slate. How to recover that original state? How to paint on it and continually rip off the pages and see ourselves again, formless and pristine; able to take a bit of all the selves that we have been and seek to be many other selves throughout our lives. It may not be a fully achievable goal in its entirety, but it is worth exploring, experimenting, and seeking alternative ways. Therein is the essence of fluidity: it is never the product that matters, but the different ways of producing.

Gabriel H. Sanchez

One:
Fused by History

Valley of the Rio Grand

In the Valley, too, we have a heart that beats
This place is not to be judged
By a mere glance
       A short stay

Here one must plant feet and
Learn to call it home
Learn to call his fellows
       Brothers—Sisters

For here too in the Valley do we have majestic trees
As tall as high rise buildings
With roach infested roots—the nightmares of BEING
       The curse of the tropical tree

Here, too, the birds make music sweet
As intermediary singers between gods and men

In the Valley palm trees wave
Their leafy arms in the wind as they sway
       Reveling in their hypnotic dance
       Laughing at our drug-induced contemplation

Below the ice-cream trucks pass
With their incessant horns
Blasting terrible renditions
       Of melodies perhaps once pleasant to the ear

In the Valley, too, do we see
Open skies smile down

And we fools sing to its unintentional
Generosity
       Stoic ever presence
           Deceiving passivity

For here, too, do tumultuous clouds hover
Above our roofs forming great visions

Of massive hands—long, thin fingers
Poised to snatch us from existence
As faces of mysterious bearded men
      Glide through the blue as fateful omens

They never pay homage to the dying sun
As humble peasants passing in front
      Of empty deserts glaring in gold
Perhaps the firing guns of border patrol
As dusty Mexicans approach with wet feet

Here in the Valley we breathe
The words of Gandhi
Whilst we eat the body of Jesus
And still we are obstructed at every corner
Suspicious eyes glaring
"There're lots'a people doing bad things 'round here"
The mid-western voice speaks to me from the migra truck
"You be sure you let us know if YOU know anything"
Fuck you, pinche Duke!

Here, too, we hear echoes of MLK
From the steps of the
      Lincoln Memorial
Whilst visions of Great Walls
line the river in dreams

Here we also feel the fire
Burn the soles of our feet
As Cuauhtémoc once endured and still
      We remain standing—you won't take my gold!
As the mob continues to grow by the Minute-
                       Man
'til the shit hits the fan
And one day a crazy, frustrated gringo enters the Pizza di Roma
restaurant on Conway Ave.
'N shouts "No matter what you do you still 'bunch-o-Mexcuns!"

(Whatever it means, this actually happened to me!)
'til the day that strung out gringo says "fuck words" and goes ballistic
Then we'll have us a billowing' bloody civil war, my friend—I dread the day

Down in the Rio Grande Valley
The air carries the weight
      Of a thousand generations

The nostrils ill-equipped to absorb
The message of philosophers past
      In solitary inhalations
Yet our hearts expand as we feast
Outgrowing the cavities of your proclivity
There is nothing left to be learned
      These fists are hard and fully formed

And from our souls a faint message gains gravitas
Fueling our expansion as we declare for ever
      That we are now the voice of the new

                        RAZA
                        COSMICA!

To MAN

MAN I think I understand
That we are here on a mission
Though prophets or healers
We have not proclaimed ourselves to be
Inevitable communicators of a message-
Transporters running long-legged
'cross the white pages
For miles on end we are

Who put these errands in our
Heads my friend?
The echoes of mad men of a now
Silent beat?
A lonely road
Visions of a body strewn besides the railroad tracks
Hiccupping to death?

For me there was a voice
From under Mexico City
The ruins watching and waiting
Sending the signals
"I'm still alive! Do not
cry for me!"
While Quetzalcoatl sits
Pleasantly above on his throne
Of Aztec pyramid bases and bones
Cemented with the flesh
of modern-day human hearts

You walk plainly past the bright
Multicolored flowers that
Drink from Lake Texcoco
Confounding you
Amazing you with their essence
How can they delight in their...
                              Differences?
How to reach them?

Difficult the task for winged and haloed wanderers
Such as you

Blameless indeed
        Pure in essence
            A legend in the making
                A virgin in evil ways
I don't blame you, you should know, but I do take heed

As for me, where do wingless ordinaries stand?
When the sky is out of reach
When the communiqué is outdated
Unappealing to the blue-ringed
Eyes that complain
"Must we really open the mind to
The possibility of learning another language?"

No one wants to hear
No one wants to listen to learn
But to recycle the old
And maintain, maintain
This is still America
This is America…
Is this still America?
Oh, it is! Good…*sigh*

We are learning something, MAN
That what we do we must
For there is something to be said
I speak of truth and
The voice of the silenced speak it too
And many tomorrows from now
We will be heard
One lonely ear
One thirsty soul
One hungry heart
Will eat of us and say:
There was once the daring
And the voice
The breath and the tongue

The heart and the soul
And there is hope yet
For MAN
For America
For Meshika

Your beloved South Texas mash
Blending and betting
On the future on nothing
Rejoicing

Our generation rescued
Through the power of the pen
By poetically diligent fingers
That say, "fuck you!"
We own the future,
In our hands resides its cradle.

The Wall Is Coming Down

The wall is coming to town
Gonna slice through
South Texas ground
Sharp, lethal, Romanesque
Gonna wound the flesh
Of victims that seek to pass
Cutting through this land
That is our home
Like an obsidian knife
Tearing through our chest
Searching to stop that heart
That beats with the movements of millennia
Migrations of our past
Are echoed in migrations of our present
The lives of men are destined
To a constant ebb and flow
No legality rules the movements
No right or wrong defines the action
Nature must take its course
Or there will eventually be war...

```
[[[[[[[[[[[[[[[[[[[[[[[[[[[[[[[[[[[[[[[[[[[[[[[[[[[[[[[[[[[[[[[[[[[[
[[[[[[[[[[[[[[[[[[[[[[[[[[[[[[[[[[[[[[[[[[[[[[[[[[[[[[[[[[[[[[[[[[[[
[[[[[[[[[[[[[[[[[[[[[[[[[[[[[[[[[[[[[[[[[[[[[[[[[[[[[[[[[[[[[[[[[[[[
[[[[[[[[[[[[[[[[[[[[[[[[[[[[[[[[[[[[[[[[[[[[[[[[[[[[[[[[[[[[[[[[[[[[
[[[[(OR)]]]]]]]]]]]]]]]]]]]]]]]]]]]]]]]]]]]]]]]]]]]]]]]]]]]]]]]]
]]]]]]]]]]]]]]]]]]]]]]]]]]]]]]]]]]]]]]]]]]]]]]]]]]]]]]]]]]]]]]]]]]]]
]]]]]]]]]]]]]]]]]]]]]]]]]]]]]]]]]]]]]]]]]]]]]]]]]]]]]]]]]]]]]]]]]]]]
]]]]]]]]]]]]]]]]]]]]]]]]]]]]]]]]]]]]]]]]]]]]]]]]]]]]]]]]]]]]]]]]]]]]
]]]]]]]]]]]]]]]]]]]]]]]]]]]]]]]]]]]]]]]]]]]]]]]]]]]]]]]]]]]]]]]]]]]]
]]]]]]]]]]]]]]]]]]]]]]]]]]]]]]]]]]]]]]]]]]]]]]]]]]]]]]]]]]]]]]]]]]]]
]]]]]]]]]]]]]]]]]]]]]]]]]]]]]]]]]]]]]]]]]]]]]]
```

Atrocities that make
The spirit rebel
Like hunting illegals
In the desert like snakes
Or shooting bullets

At a man holding rocks
Calling it self-defense

(but you neglect to state
that he never threw at you, Mr. Migra!)
The wall is coming down on us
It's making its tour
All the way from Germany where it fell flat by the weight of its
own hate

It's making its grand debut passing itself off as new
Making a canvas for Chicanos to paint
Vatos and Rucas claiming the page
Picks and axes and voices and pens

We'll take the streets to the end
Shouting across these South Texas towns
The wall is coming down
THE WALL IS COMING DOWN
THE WALL IS COMING DOWN!

Moctezuma's Ghost

See the kingdom fall, see...
The dangers materializing
Like a filthy curtain of doom
Falling to shut out the lights!

Darkness presumes its eminence
Upon all souls good or bad
This tragedy befalls not just one
But all men, women, children...

Children of lesser gods cry
In the dawn of this new city
With murky rivers of blood
Where their futures run gushing in haste

As the spears break and the ground quakes
Remember that we are but flowers
Stepped on, crushed and bent out of shape
But like nopal we pride ourselves in our roots

Let the metal beasts thrash about
We hold through to the end of time
Like underdogs in a one-sided fight
Like the roots of a broken nopal

Motecuzoma, believer of myths
Rest your soul in your wandering
Lament no more, for what occurred here
Was not your doing, nor God's but of men

To God we are not like grains of sand but rain clouds upon the
desert
Our tears of blood have summoned life stronger
We were never meant to extinguish
Our clay bodies absorbed the spear of annihilation!

It is true you could have spared us all

This pain of agonizing loss

By a mere swapping away of the vision of Cortez as a god
And let us see you walk again and be a man among men

Yet as we hold on to meet
Your haunting spirit absolved of its wrongs
The remembrance of you bearing the weight of the sun
Lighter still than your guilt, strengthens us

And we grow strong...

And we hold on

Free Isn't Freedom (For George W. Bush)

Thinner, drier, dehydrated, dead
The minds of my generation
Uninspired, endangered
Consumed in the fires of this modern
Mainstream nation

Silent   Alone   Lost
In the eternities of internet connections
Talking loudly
Saying nothing

Reality TV
Our ambassador to the world
MTV our church
Hollywood our Mecca
Disney World Paradise!

But God don't fit in this SUV
We're goin' over mountains
And 'cross the sea
While Buddha HOWLs his poetry
to eternity without me

One last time I'll be hungry
For reality a taste
Only to satisfy the emptiness
With a meal of 99 cents

Yet the hunger remains, though the belly is full
Though Freedom Fries
From my orifices froth forth and fall out

It's okay
It's not real
Nothing Freud couldn't heal
With a quick hit, snort, line, bump--white teeth pealed, grinning
involuntarily

Forgetting my starvation
In my stomach…
Nah, in my soul!

It's not real it's not real

Not the hunger
that rumbles at my heels
That I walk
a path outside
the program box

Not the hunger in my liver
that I drink the world
To toxicity 'n die
Of happy life-poisoning

Not the hunger in my lungs
That I hold my breath
Until the night—mare
Of modern humanity disappears
Or I collapse and spare
Myself of this anyway

Not the hunger in my mind
That I find reason to believe again
To preach to the trees and stones
And anyone who will listen that there is Hope
For mankind after all

Not the hunger in my lobes
That I can turn on the TV
And not be violated with banality 'n
Narcissism-fanaticism-fascism-intolerance-unreality 'n lies

That pundits speak because they know the truth
Not because the ends justify the means
'N mushroom clouds could be hanging over cliffs
In the Rocky Mountains and off the edge of the Empire State building

Not the hunger in my eyes
That I may open them to see
The President Turn the Other Cheek
To deny an Eye for a bloody Eye
… 'n then some

Not the hunger in my fingers
That I may conquer Evil within
To lift a fist not in hate
        But in love
Not in aggression
        But in friendship
Not in haste responding absent-thoughtfully
        But after deliberate deliberation

It's no easy contention
My brothers, my sisters,
The children of My Generation
To awake from sleep and seek change
A hostile world stares back at all truth tellers…

But fear not to shun the box that can't save us
And step firmly into the really real world
Rejoicing while we let the pen tell the story
Of this new generation forged in truth and poesy

WMD Brain Freeze

All I can do for solace is
Retreat to my coat
Seek the warmth of my chest
And wait and hope that construction is delayed
As Fox & Friends paint the new landscape
Across the horizons of the world's nations
A forest of Atom bomb seeds blooming
Mushroom Cloud Chandeliers looming
        Nice decorations
        Hanging on the arms of
        God's avatars in a fight
        Illuminating—   Fuck the sun!
They say, "We beat the Russians"
"Reagan brought down the Wall"
"The Cold War Is Over MAN!
Annihilation's prevented
We can live and work in peace and tranquility
Safe and secure"
        Meanwhile Annihilation waits smiling sinister
        In the desperate minds of little men
        And our leaders encourage us to
        Shop and forget
        No one dies in vain
        Patriots buy American-made...
It's the fight on the RIGHT side of history
The free world is taking care of its own
Just give us your bodies and minds
Just jump when we say
Threat high—level raised color red
The color of North Korea
The color of China Communism
The color of Al Qaeda's imminent threat
Rising stars against the WEST
What you say there non-government entity?
Little man of no significance 'cause you weren't "elected"
"The world is about to end? I'll tell YOU when it'll end"
        It's true nothing is written

The future is being shaped
By the present—the president
Though the wisest time tense is the past
And she said life goes on, my friend
No WMDs can interfere, for none were found

The Iraq War Is OVER, MAN!
Paranoid pariah
Agent of destabilization!
Agitator of fears now forgotten
Must you remind 'da 'merican people of their
fears?!!!!!!!!!!!!!!!!!!!!!!!!!
We look toward the bright fu-
ture!!!
          "But bombs were made to explode no matter who got
'em!!!!!!!!!!!

                    Warheads were made for destruction
                    Bombs are patient grim reapers
                    Of our civilizations   ((   )
                    The great equalizers_____)
                    If not Saddam's stockpiles,
                    Our trigger-happy fingers
                    Can cancel time on a flinch
                    And so we seize to exist

                    Get up from there MAN
              and listen to yourself! For once in life
        look at yourself and see your world for the first time
         Outside the programming box what beautiful skies
          Living in the shadows of mushroom cloud trees
                    flaming at their tops
                      Lanterns of gods
                     The brilliance of our
                          Humanity
                          Awaiting
                          the fall
              !!!!!!!!!!!!!!!!!!!!!!!!!!!!!!!!!
              !!B!!!!!!!!!!!O!!!!!!!!!!!O!!!!!!!!!!!M!!

Monkey See

I got to go out there to the open
I must face the cold
Like a newborn first time
Citizen of the world

My hands have come free
From the shackles of bondage
To repetitious consumption
And my eyes have seen the vicious war

All weapons have clicked to converge
Above my mind of sediment
The progression from peace is purged
Officials never make it official

A lie rings throughout
The light boxes of the globe
The giant is smug
I alone must fight Goliath

Like zombies they move about in SUVs
Gas guzzling their monotonous ruin
Mountain climbing, pond gliding
Yet SUVs don't bow to Earth

They think the Hummer will
Save them from destruction
But its blood is oil, a sure chain
For the enslavement of all

Comfortable life trips
to Disneyland, eight to five
Sheep of society smiling in the distance
Holding a telescope the suffering
Is contagious so just close your eyes and
See No Evil

An Arab hates
An African starves
A Chinese is red
A Soviet stands in Czech

A South American rebels
A Central American is oppressed
A Mexican struggles to his feet
Americans watch reality TV

Closure comes with sleep
Freedom waits in dreams
In the meantime face the heat
Of insurgency running loose

Just say no, just drink booze
Just give to the church
Just confess every Sunday
Just believe in your president
And look the other way

But before our pools of blood
Have transformed to pools of oil
Be sure to catch my sway
As your eyes I do persuade
To see the world today...SHROUDED IN HORROR

War America

Where are the poets of America?
Who's talking of our realities?
Are we broken mirrors unable to present the full view
Relegated to talking of cocks and cunts
Of haloed angels roaming the streets
Getting Jack-ed-off On the Road
Only hinting at a discontent?

Where were those heroes of American poetry
When the Fox network declared that we were the enemy
That we are illegal
That we are criminal
O'rielly don't embrace no colored man no matter how patriotic

And where were the heroes of poetic America
When they said we invaded as if war hungry monsters bent on
destruction
Who started this war?
If not the middle of the nation where the meat-n-potatoes started
Tastin' better cuz the Mexcuns were tilling the soil at slave wages
but then wanted to bring their mothers and their fathers and their
sisters and their brothers and
The All-American boys strapped on their hoods in a panic,
in a violent Minute
Calling themselves patriotic,
tragic figures out on the quest to preserve America
And they do it happily if it will quash a lowly immigrant in the
Arizona dessert
Or drown the down-trodden in the toxic waters of the Rio Grande
stream
Fighting as if for anything other than a nation of immigrants...

Who called this war America?
Who if not you, for you started all wars that have torn us apart?
Who started the War On Drugs
If not America in the intent to flood the Panthers out of the
streets with crack cocaine?

Who started the war on illegal immigration?
Though ragged sailors were your fathers
Who crossed a larger stream?
Yet they didn't apply for no citizenship
And they didn't ask but took
And they didn't work for all but for themselves

And they didn't first build on what was here but first destroyed
And then hung up bows and arrows on their air conditioned walls
as relics of a forgone era as if saying "Ah, fate. She is a fickle lady."
And an Indian shed a tear on the TV and you thought wow that
was the Ingun way, so in touch with mother Earth that they
would cry if they saw the garbage in the streets

America you are obsessed with war
You have declared war on I-literacy
But the dead presidents make no tours down to the barrios and
the ghettos
And the schools barely have paint on walls
And the teachers don't teach but indoctrinate
And the history is absent and Columbus is a hero
And slavery's ghost is dead...right?
And reverse racism is real! YOU try being a white in this America, I dare you.
And Affirmative Action has eradicated poverty
And the jails hold equal numbers of whites and colored and—
WAIT!
This America doesn't exist

Here in America there'll never be peace
There'll never be love
There'll always be prejudice
There'll always be war

THIS is America love it or leave it...

                                    Or change it

But with change always travels conflict
And so the war isn't over, America
The war has just started.

In Resonance to Serj Tankian's Comment on Civilization

Part I

I am an American
I hail from a proud people
From all parts of these continents

I am a citizen of the world
My brothers and sisters
Have been among the oldest civilizations

I am a citizen of the western hemisphere
I am a citizen...without borders
I am a citizen...not a denomination

I am an American in the full sense of the word
I have felt much of the suffering
In the narrow streets of this hemisphere

I am a citizen of the world
I have died a billion deaths
In wars for freedom, wars for oppression, wars for war

I am an American in the full sense of the word
I have never been a Hispanic
I don't know how to be Latino

I have never been a Mexican American
I have never been Indian...
My ancestors never came from India

I am not a NATIVE AMERICAN
Nobody has ever been native
To any part of the world in isolation

I am Native of Earth
All people have always been, are, and will be...
NATIVE to Mother Earth

I am not, yet I am
Is it truly a dichotomy?
Or is it simply flights of fancy?

Is it incongruity?
Or is it mere simplicity?
To be not, yet be?

The ginger bread man
Never felt superior to his fellows
Until he was cut from the dough...

Amid flowing rivers of Indian blood
In obstructed European veins...

It's all in vain.
To think about justice
The walls of our city have cracked
         down to memories.
Who can avenge the gods
When our bones have eroded?
Time ended a long time ago, and hope went with it,
And now no one can find us engaged
If not through a lowly Facebook page

Waking the Dead

Get up from that bed and wake up, MAN!
We are not eternal! -CECR

I see people walking and talking
Living their lies dying their dreams
Some don't look more alive
Than dead relatives in old graves

Some look alive only because
The glimmer of false pretense
Still sparkles in their eyes
You can see it on their whitened teeth

...on their fruitless claim of ownership...
Over their lives, over their bodies
Inspired not by knowledge or certainty
Inspired by the mere fact that they breathe

They forget that only blood runs through our veins
That the air in our lungs is temporary
For with a whimper we exhale and seize to be
Such is the obvious mystery of human frailty

Some hang their hopes and aspirations
On titles and false pretensions
On kissing ass and buying whatever is expensive
Seeking brand names to legitimize their own names

It's a sinister complacency
A tragic tale of suicide
by default thinking
A global story of genocide at the hands of our T.V.s

When you fail to act [YOU WILL BE ACTED UPON!]

Walking with corpses, the un-waking zombies
Eat our brains with their ignorance and our hearts with blind rituals
And yet, aren't angels and saints
Made of these?

Brush Strokes (Of the End of the World)

Brush strokes
Paintbrushes dripping blood
The picture of the world
Formed and nurtured by war

The floodgates of distortion
Of lies and half-truths have opened
Attack! Attack! Attack!
Preemptive privilege is the right!

Stomp those cockroaches coming under…the door
Immigrants—criminals—terrorists!
We cannot accept the brown paint
Creeping on the southern canvas

War on terror
War on drugs
War on illegals
War on immigrants!

We bring your new Aztec tragedy
An Achilles Heal of your own
Ignorance of the past transformed
To repeat itself as the end nears

As Quetzalcoatl approaches earth in the serpent raft
Upon the vastness of the ocean that is the sky blue
You hate me and press harder your foot
Upon my neck to keep me down

You should fear now—get to know fear
You think you know war
Killing our chance to send Quetzalcoatl back
By tearing our body in two as you…rid yourself of me

As you weaken the body
Laying it open on a field of flowers
As a lover waiting for your love to bloom
As fragile as those flowers you exterminated with bio—
Warfare is coming!

Quetzalcoatl ain't no god

Cortez incarnate
He comes for conquest and we're the bait
For you to hate and persecute

So we may stand on shaky ground
Like man-made islands
Standing on swampy waters—divided
Aztec incarnate

We're doomed to sink into extinction
As the prophecy of the messiah fulfills itself
The imminent coming of the one who will rule
The one who will strike the brush of war against us

As we pray for his coming
As we welcome his hidden intentions
As we pardon his anonymous origins
And call him god—ancestral promise

Quetzalcoatl! – Jesus Christ!
Aliens disguised as deities
In their strange ships
To exploit your Achilles heel of hate

In the name of national security
Patriot acts
War on the terrorists!
Those criminals, illegals —   dirty

brown

immigrants!

Barrio Flowers

We
Entrenched here
In this battle zone
(in this barrio, this ghetto)
Like flowers in a field
Plucked at the randomness
Of desire

You
Blazing brown roses
Don't make me torch my fire
Don't tempt my eyes
Swaying there
Like dancers in the air

Like reaching to the sky
With arms outstretched
Offering your prayers as you beg
For mercy from this psycho—
                              I'll cut you!
From your blooming cycle

I
Barrio flowers in my trek
Scattering about
Spreading their seed
I clip-clip-clip to your dismay
And with your corpses I fill my bouquet

And if a thorn you expose
I'll chant your defeat
Like Coyolxauhqui
Lying dismembered at my feet
Proclaiming your agony after death—
                              Oh, deepest regret
With your tongue sticking out of your mouth,
                              Fleeing
Your tragically broken skull

Bush Era Love

Because everybody is just one really good fuck away
From cooling all their shit
All aggressions are within reach to become pacified
All nuclear warheads will rot as presidents 'n dictators get head
like never before
Every little man in vice president chairs with their misery could
Cease 'n desist, desist all torture 'pon the bodies of
The deserts as someone just eats the anger out
Through his butthole
Condi would say Mr. Bush, it's been a pleasure
But now there's another BUSH I must assist!
And she'd fuck half the MIDDLE
          East
Of where she sits and seduces the sickness of war
'N she'd grow wings 'n fly 'n an angle face would supplant the
cold looks 'n calculated
          expressions 'n cemented-firm-facial-features
'N all would be well,
GOD would be proud
G.O.D. would stand for "Grateful Of Dick"
'N God in his reverie decides he'd might as well cancel that whole
Apocalypse business—Armageddon—and just cool it
And He'd look for some luscious goddess tail
or Gay God cock and
the Universe would grow tits 'n fuck the neighbors 'n
Peace would be achieved, humanity understood
Time 'n Space retired to eternal ecstasies

Search for the Burning Spear

There are pains that linger in her
Like feelings that yell at the gates
At the gatekeeper and threaten to riot out
Good and evil, which are undistinguishing and
Undistinguished

Following the theme that she was forced to follow,
Civilization walked away from the rain in the night
One night, when, for no apparent reason,
Our voices sang of old spirits
That would come to take the reins.

Singing the tunes of the dead,
Why is it so dreadful to tread through the halls
And the caves, and the sewers, and the backdoors
Of the present that lead to the past?

Tell me something if you will, well-meaning spirit of old,
Can civilization wander to the past with you and share the tree
Over the shade and sing the melody of the parody of
today?
Can she tread with you, Great Spirit of old,
To the perilous canyons of your flourishing civilization
That was mother to millions and, to the same,
                                    their grave?
And there seek out and attain the burning spear
To slash and burn to ashes those she calls maggots
For their blind consumption

I want to see her in full attire
to sing the hymn of peace
Then yell out the cry of war
Followed by torching battles
                    (to mend the breach)
Against the tight-sealed enemy in his plastic suit.

Civilization Petrification

Civilization is caving.
It's falling apart.
Breaking up into a million pieces,
each containing groups of people stuck in their own ways.
Refusing to give an inch, a centimeter, a millimeter.
Refusing to give themselves the uncomfortable feeling that is
freedom.
True freedom not only from the dangers of repressive acts or their
rights
infringed upon by others.
But the freedom from all which includes themselves.
They are their own jailer.

We close the door to growth when this growth
involves applying the same level of fairness and honesty to the
lives of others who are vastly different than us.
That is death.
That is stagnation.
That is the dry bearing in the wheel
that eventually brings the whole contraption to a screeching halt
then paralyzes it until it is obsolete.
Don't be the dried out ball bearing.
Lubricate your mind so that you can
flow with the swing of things coming and going.

World of Conquest

Like spontaneous combustion
Are man's actions but some of us—still
Struggle with heavy weights dragging our soles
And an ancestral experience
Burdening our impoverished soul.

The tired feet of these clandestine thinkers
Are their only prize in this world of conquest,
Where only mindless action
Disguised and proclaimed as righteous
Justifies evil deeds:

The pursuit of senseless agitations,
The condemnation of our youth to wars of oblivion,
The infection of bullets and bombs
It's a new day,
        An old body,
                Sensing the stench of a dying sun.
The fifth sun ended with our fathers by invasion
Our mothers nurtured the ashes of our wounded spirit
Never again shall we let them fool us
We are one for all or we are nothing

And we sit here oozing out our quiet indignations,
For history begets history
Wars repeat
People continually victimized
Who will pay for these transgressions?

And we remain here waiting to explode into flaming torches,
To begin to rage against the beast in full protest
[under a lid of lead]
Shouting deftly for revolution…

I Am The Bridge

"You've separated yourself!
You've put yourself at opposite ends of the American stream!"
That's what he said to me
But he's wrong
I am the bridge!
I am the voice that rises from the river's edge
Clamoring, claiming, clinging onto an identity
My identity
Not that which you have given unto me
But the one I chose when my eyes where shown the light
Like a born-again Christian
I was a born-anew Chicano
Chaotically poised and tempered
Contrasting and conflicting against the social scripts
Even as a Chicano I cannot resist
To transcend the expectations
Of without and within
To always seek to be the fluid
That fluxes from the American cup to the Mexican cup
From the minority cup to the alien cup
Being and not being
The waters of the river that streams to demark definitions
And the bridge above it that holds both worlds together.

Flux

Who's talking of our identity?
I welcome the challenge.
As a Chicano Mestizo
I am undefined
Though the census
Presumes to know me
better than I know myself
it labels me
something I know little about
it says I'm something
other than that
which I know myself to be:
A child of the stars
A product of a collision
Of worlds that meshed
Together to make
That which courses through
The veins of all my people
Regardless of the color of our skin,
The place of our birth
The language that spits off our tongues
We are ever changing
Chicanos, Mestizos, Mulatos
Mixed blood whites, browns, reds, blacks...
All representative and
None representing alone
This is a true existence
Experiencing arrays of perspectives,
Realities, locations, and struggles
All leading to a true American Melting Pot
A Chicano fluidity of the self
Changing with the times over and over again

Two:
An Internal Flux

Yearning

Yearning...that my universe exploding in your space
Creates constellations to decorate your face
Like an unstoppable force
Meeting an object with open arms
Greeting, seeking their depths in each other
Accelerating heartbeats and breaths
Sweat beads and sweet bread after the deed
Tenderizing these moments
Tantalizing these dreams
Wishing you here with me
I cling onto these irrational thoughts
That you will come back to my bed
Irrational because you are dead
Your shadow sitting next to me
Calling me crazy for telling you sweet things
But sanity is the sickness
For I still feel your touch
And your taste still clings to my tongue
Anchored by your sweet scent now tattooed on my airways
Like cave paintings hanging tenaciously
To walls defying time and the elements
I cling to you in life defying the great divide
Wishing for you in death...
Wishing for your breath

Father

Father
I don't like you becoming me
Because as sure as the sun shines on a clear sky
I am becoming you

You do the things I used to do
You say the things I used to say
I say and do like you in return
Not by choice but by
A sick way of this life that switches our roles to confuse us
To land us in an unconquerable cycle
Chasing each other and each other's ghosts
You of the past, I of the present
Both of the future

The future, perhaps what gave you nightmares
When you requested "leave the light on when you close my door"
Requesting like a child, afraid of dark shadows
When I of the dark am no longer afraid

What are you afraid of?
The darkness of the mind
That resembles the darkness of the grave?
That unknown consequence of death

Father I don't like you becoming me
Because as you become me
You don't resemble what I may be
But the me of yesteryear

Me the child that fears
Me the fetus where life still may not hold
Me the infant suddenly dead
How? Who knows?
Here this second gone the next

In me you regress
As me you'll search again
For the flavors of dirt
In the soil underneath the orange trees

Father the tree has withered in the winter of its days
But below the surface the roots remain
The Lila keeps sprouting leaves
On the arms of its ghost in your cold absence

And we who are like orange trees
We have roots that rot in the ground
And branches that give way to ice-cold breath
Perhaps the reason I don't like you
Becoming me because as me
You will shrivel and die...

Gone dead

She lay in her sweat
Piss released
As death choked her life
Taking the promise of tomorrow
In her womb now cold
Babies still unborn
Laid down to dream
Under the grapefruit tree
The family's own pet cemetery
Here today
Eat drink
Gone tomorrow when we wake
To find stiffness in her place
A memory of what once was
A life snuffed
Like the fire of a cigarette
Dropped before the final drag
My image in the mirror
Remembering her life
Burying her in a dark hole
In the ground with sweat
Trickling off our brow
Mimicking tears falling from our eyes
The tears we felt inside
But did not manifest
We were at peace with destiny
Hers today ours tomorrow
My hands dry on a towel
I walk in drunken stupor
Her image on my mind
Lying in the ground I dug
Sending her home to God
As we remain
Waiting for our turn
To meet our final hour
When we, too, will feel
The earth's embrace
As we lay down to sleep
Eternally

Landscapes of Eternity

Man is born alone
and so, too, does he die alone
Perhaps this is why
when he falls in love
he feels an emotion
so powerful surge within him
to the degree that he believes himself
capable of defying the limits of mortality
the sheer force of an unstoppable destiny
and the awesome powers of God Himself
in his feeble attempts at circumventing
the certainty of a fate that binds him
to an ultimate loneliness in life.
And so only his solitude in death
provides the illusion of company
to traverse the long and dejected road
which passes through the landscapes of eternity...

Nothing Lasts Forever (The Cosmic Escape)

I love you
I wanna make love to you
I wanna find myself in your paradise
and throw blows at the seams until they break
and we are engulfed in a sea of passion
so vast that neither of us could hope
to swim to a shore, for none exists
and so our sole recourse
is to hold each other tightly and succumb to the flood
which pulls us down as we drown in its sweet ecstasy.
So do not dwell on the unforseen
Do not fear our respective capacities to falter
from our stated promises of love
Nothing lasts forever...
But while we have each other and this love
let us rejoice and celebrate this fleeting union
on this existential plane where all things perish
and hope that our souls can catch a falling star by the tail and ride
it across the sky
in a cosmic escape from non-existence
and perhaps in that way we can be together
forever without the fear of betraying our love
because creatures of light can never take each other for granted,
lest they be willing to risk
obscuring the fires that brighten the heavens...

Lineage of Man

Who is that on that floor
Two feet knocking
High heels rockin'
Butt cheeks swaying
Back and forth
Side to side
What simplicity
This humanity of mine
Taken in by shapes and forms
By sounds that imply woman
Passing by
Where is the internal sensor
The antenna to detect
Defect
Wretchedness
None to be found in all of us
Men
Only a pair of primitive eyes
A dull, easily amused brain
Senses like
No like
This be the roots of humanity
These are the fabric of destiny
I think I hear the footsteps again
Click-clack, click-clack
Check out that rack
Mama I got what you need
You got the egg I got your seed
When someone kills that switch
That makes us want to fuck
They kill off the human race
Funny thing about the lineage of man
It's mostly magically based on luck

Obsession

You, object of my obsession not desired
For a permanence but for perpetual unattainability—you
As long as I desire you I long for you...
If I had you for myself entirely, I'd have killed your magic

When you are mine I will have no more wish
To have you with me, for it is now that you are
My obsession, my object of desire
On your chest I find fertile mountains

As I delight my senses kissing your peaks
Rubbing against your warm valley
Pictures of your original state of being
Are formed in my head day and night

And I cannot stop the machine in my head
That makes me yearn, yearn for your touch
I relive those days when I reach for you
To possess you like a hungry child reaches for his mother's breast

But in suckling on your flesh, I feel no kinship
Only your succulent nipples take me away
To spaces non-reached by gods or men
A potent injection of deafening ejaculation

O, I swear to you, I surely will go to hell
And burn for my unceasing burning for you
In my lustful wishing to have you touching me,
Holding me inside you, calling my name, I die

Panting and hoping that you
Elevate me over and beyond the darkness
That emptiness of the sky behind the stars
I will surely die...

Before I get to redeem my spirit, before I
Get to make the wrong things right

This obsession for you is tearing me
Tearing at my soul and I feel like an animal

Like an animal I hunger—starve—for your flesh,
Uneasy pain, unceasing passions, regretful solutions
To possess you and possess you with vigor—
Without delay...

And when the consumption of this sumptuous feast of you
Is ensued and then presumed finalized, I shall desire you once
again
I will be one to say that no love can be existent
In the passion that I feel burning for you

Such is the truth of my desire for you, so I shall request
(No, I shall require!) that you lay...
On my ceremonial bed once again so that I may...
Tear your chest with my seething teeth in a frenzy

And in this frenzy of wanton craving for your flesh I shall
Eat out your heart to quell the stirring in my loins,
To drive away the animal and be a man again with the desire
For you obscured and extinguished like the flames of a raging
fire...

>Finitely covered with dirt...
>And I will be saved

Song of Love/Song of Death

If I could sing you
A song
It would be a magic
Of thoughts and sound.

It would be a revelation
Of elementary responses
To all our humanly questions.

I would touch nothing less than
Your very soul
While imagining our bodies
In a tangled ritual of the flesh.

If I could sing you a song
It would be the only one
I know
The one that comes from beyond;
That melts icy sentiments
And burns dry sensations.

In my song I would sing of you
For no other thing inspires me so;
To feel such alien emotions
In a heart of rancid notions
That for years discarded
Love's truth—until
My eyes fell upon you.

So from now until forever
In our hearts, our ears, our eyes
Our lips and all our senses
My song would play as incessant
As the waves of the ocean that dwell
Eternally in the bowels of a conch shell.

And in each lyric

The intuitive knowledge
Will be felt
That all the things that make us
Imperfect
Are justified
Because from error we come
And with music it is nullified.

So caress my voice
As I sing to you
Let me know what I can do
To let every note
Liberate us both.

And let me carry you
Like a feather in the wind that blows
To the eternal bliss
Of the highest reverie
Where our bodies might only be
Distant memories
Somewhere _____ the grass
                \ beneath /

Held-there-while-we—S
                    E
                    E
                    P
                Beyond our planet's grasp.

I Wait

The days pass by so slowly thinking of you.
Yearning for you.
Wondering if when I do get to touch you again,
will your body respond to me like it did before?

Will I hear the sweet music from your lips calling me,
saying my name,
urging me to finally come in
as if entering a holy place where our love is safe and eternal?

I wonder if I will be limited
in my expressions of desire for your love,
or if you will let me have free range over your prairie
to be and act in any way I may be so inspired?

I feel you here now as if we never parted ways.
I suffer in your absence but relish this slowly burning passion
inside me
like a fire that starts innocently on a leaf
and then consumes an entire forest.

So, too, this fire in me is waiting
to erupt upon your skin
in an explosion of sweet and tender love...
I wait.

I count the minutes,
reliving the past,
dreaming of things to come
...wrapped in your arms.

Butterfly in Amber

She exists in a world of perfection and beauty
like a butterfly trapped in amber long ago.
But I know that isn't her.
She is alive and real
and on the same path to discover
the hidden truths of life and the universe,
and God Himself as all humanity.
And this truth about her helps me see
when I stare at her picture and think I have seen enough.

I know now that I have been blind
like most men are when stricken by
the thrills of having before them a monument
to womanly wonders such as she possesses.
I yearn every day to have her attention and derive from her
the matter that I use to produce
the thread of poetry that shoots from my hands
like the fictional superhero shoots spider web.

But I realize that this is a selfish motive
that she is not a concept but a woman
of varied levels of complexity
like the closed petals of a fragrant flower.
However, I don't want this inspiration to end.
I want to write tributes to her magnificence
until I die or until my well runs dry. Yet I
worry that she will grow weary of my words
and believe them to be false.

If only I could assure her they are not.
They have no design other than
to please the muse who inspired them.
So let me invite you to indulge me in this fantasy
and come along in mind and spirit, at least,
to this place where you are the sun that brightens my days.

In this world you rule the nights as well

for and at your pleasure.
Here you are the weaver of dreams,
the goddess that grants life and death.
In this world you come and go at your convenience and I,
your high priest, await your return with faith,
with eyes closed and hands together over my chest;
waiting to receive a revelation
giving my words of worship your happy benediction.
Here I wish to stay forever,
for here poetry and romance never die...

Lovers Born Anew

Who can claim they know you?
when your heart never spoke to them,
when their kisses evaporated on the surface of your skin without
ever landing anywhere close to your heart.
Who can say they know you?
when your love never touched their souls?
when your eyes still glow with the power of a newborn sun wait-
ing to find its living being yearning for its warmth to bathe in.
In this I am not wrong
I love you despite all others come and now gone.
No need for explanations,
I know that you're the one.
In my eyes no one has ever touched you
you are pure as a baby born new
In my heart no one can love you like i do
because i, too, began life the day i met you.

Aztec Love

Hearts and hands hang to the chest:
I've felt you near me
Feeding my expansive soul
With your subtle sweetness

Serpent feathers and raft of snakes:
I spent two years waiting
For you to take me away

Pagan gods in their heads
But no pagan minds:
I've ripped open my chest
For I long to feel your touch
Upon my beating heart.

Wrap your hands around
That living jewel
It pumps with life
Only since I met you.

Falling sun chasing
The moon:
My struggle continues until
I have you with me

Bestow upon me light
And darkness
With
Your eyes of life
And
Your lips of death.

I'll never end the
Fight until I've merged
The sun and moon into
A perfect unity—until
I've drank of you and you've

Drank of me

> Until we've secured the eternal
> Life of our love, for
> We have the thirst of the gods

My Paintings

My words are
my paint,
my poems
my rendering of you.

Like an artist
paints his subject
on a canvas,
so too I paint
the essence of you
in these lines.

So tonight sleep.
Sleep and dream
that my words
envelop you like a shield against all adversity.

And when you awake may you find
these paintings
by your bedside
and see them once again and think of me
and smile.

The Freckles on Your Skin

How can you think of my love spread out and misplaced?
How could you ever doubt that I am yours?
I long for you.
I've dreamt of you.
In my fantasies i've held you in my arms
in an embrace far more wonderful than before.

I want to give you that which only you inspire in me.
A touch that burns with my passion.
A kiss that lingers on your skin long after we've been together.
No questions. No reservations. No thoughts of a tomorrow with-
out you.

Only the moment in your eyes.
My name falling from your lips.
Your breath caressing me as I disappear between your fingers
and become a cluster of freckles on your chest.

Whenever you want me,
all you need to do is stretch out your arm and,
with a sweet caress upon those specks,
summon me once again.

I'll appear before you
out of that time we shared in our youth
where I was inebriated by the nature of your beauty
which is more profound than the oceans and the source of it
more valuable than any sunken treasures of the deep.

In My Hands

I feel you slipping from my hands,
slipping away into that dark abyss
where friends, acquaintences and
once love-interests go to be forgotten,

bypassed for, perhaps,
a better alternative.
And I ask myself:
does that man exist in your midst?

Does he see your eyes in still pictures
and feel them staring into his soul?
Does he think of you and feel your words still burning his heart
with passion
like when you told me "I really like you...Gabriel".

Does he write you
sweet words of love
Even though he doesn't
have you face to face?

I think of these things
when the minutes and the hours pass
and your absence becomes palpable,
thick like quicksand and I am...

...enveloped in torturing moments
of agony without your rescuing words
that simply say "Hello,"
and then all is made well again.

Then I can breath romance again and let my fingers
caress your inner mind searching for your core;
that which is innate, primordial; that which with childlike inno-
cence
follows my words of devotion to a land where dreams come true;

A land where we awake to find souls kissing, yet they possess no
lips;
where those souls form perfect unions and intercourses
in the absence of frail bodies that eventually wither and die and
cannot
carry the soul and its awesome power and splendor.

I look over my shoulder.
Are you there?
Is that the sound of your footsteps
following my dedication at its heels?

If the pain that filled your heart persists,
then let these be the terms that exorcise those demons of empti-
ness and angst
and let your spirit immerse itself in the plenteous source
of my inspiration until it be fulfilled.

Your Nectar

The streets are wet.
It's grey outside.
Liquid drops are crashing on my window panes
Like miniature kamikaze airplanes.

In my head your name crashes on my sides mimicking the rain,
flooding my thoughts
with you.

Where are you?
I limp across the room in my loneliness like a lion wounded in
battle
dying for want of his lioness' breath.

Where are your breasts? Breasts which suckled new life but
which once preserved my youth.

Where is your sweet caress?
I wander across this dry and lonely desert of life in search of
your nectar hidden away to some sacred spot of this world which
might reserve a tiny sample of your essence to revive me.

You are the Earth.
Your disposition dictates the fate of living things.

Come lift this drought from my shoulders
drench my tree again with the showers of your love.

It is that sweet nectar which you possess
that, like the rain replenishes the ground on which my flowers
bloom,
you give life to my heart which once had died
with your goodbye.

But with you I am revived
With you I am renewed
With you I feel my heart again
With your name coursing in my veins...

When Your Eyes Are Looking

When your eyes are looking, clouds form patterns in the sky
of lovers' bliss, hands in hands,
lips to lips...hearts to hearts locked in a kiss.

When your eyes are looking, flowers bloom at odd hours filling
rooms and closets, gardens and lonely hearts that brood in tandem
seeking their Love's reward.

When your eyes are looking
I write sweet words of love while my soul sings
Hoping you take notice
Wishing you here with me

When your eyes are looking
I blush not because I fear your gaze, not because
the power of your soul takes note of mine own...but because I
fear the certainty that those eyes will shut forever as all eyes do
one day close and die.

When your eyes are no longer looking
I will not know what window to open
and look for it again.
So on that day your soul
will be lost to me,
and so that day will be
my last until in heaven we meet.

Memories Soaked In Brine

I don't know if you know this in your heart
but let your mind understand
that I've had your name on my tongue all day.

I don't speak it to anyone yet because im afraid
that if I open my mouth even briefly
your name would fly away like a bird
mimicking the spirit that hides in the person you are.
A person coated in layers, shielding your core,
the true you that belongs among the angels in the sky.

Please tell your mind that I am beginning to remember you again,
for the memory of you, too, has been coated-over
deep in the recesses of my mind
ever since you walked out of the chambers of my heart.

But, yes, I rejoice today!
I want to shout it out at the birds over my head
and at the dead compartments of my remembrances
so as to reawaken them with the happy happenstance of the re-
turn of you.

Yes…now I remember you.
You are the one that walked away one long ago day.
You are the one who was always there under my skin, permeating
everything.
And so like Joel slept and was reawakened with a spotless mind
only to find and rediscover the one he'd lost in memory's brine—
so, too, are you my Clementine.

To A-muse...you

I feel your essence entering me through the pores of my skin.
I feel an incredible need to be in your presence
and have eyes meet eyes and introduce our souls.

I want to feel the fire from deep inside you
consuming my every layer of skin, flesh, and bone
into ashes until I am lifted by a gust of wind
and whisked up to the cold atmosphere, where I can freeze
and there exist in orbit 'till the end of eternity
with the pleasure of having been touched by you
still coursing through my every single particle.

But in my stead, let this poem be the messenger
that greets you and gives word on my behalf.
Let this messenger create a space in your heart
where orchids bloom not nurtured by the rays of our star
but by the bits of my spirit on which these verses feed.

And one happy day I know these flowers
will fill that space so fully that
with a simple sigh and a thought of me
I will be summoned to your side
to tend to that garden
with the life-giving warm waters
of my everlasting love.

To the Luteus Flower Blooming In My Window Sun

Your beauty radiates across the Earth
like a beacon touching all,
incinerating the passions in men's hearts
in ways none of us knew we could be so inspired.

Words cannot describe the mystery in your eyes...
the body shivers, the language is absent,
the tongue twists inside the mouth—then becomes immobilized,
and the air cowers in my lungs as if afraid to stand before your
shimmering beauty.

For your friendship, a man could walk across the deserts of the
world
without water or sustenance, but nourished simply by a mere
picture of you.
For your love, I would grind the stars to dust until they filled an
ocean beachfront where you could play... your simplicity revealed.

And at that stardust bed may you lay
and shine your light throughout the universe
to guide the way for streaking comets darting across the sky
and fallen angels alike, on their way to Earth to worship you.

Wailing

I heard a wailing down by the shore.
It was my lover calling my name.
I didn't hear you at first, O, singing flower.
But now the tentacles of my tree have awakened again.
Again I begin to feel you building nests
for birds to sing in and make love.
Again I feel the roots of your flower tickling my trunk.
The leaves begin to bud again on my writing branch.
Do you see them? Do you feel my poetry
running its lines through your hair
as my fingers would if you were here?
But my sweet Onsidium, I am the tall yet immovable tree.
You are the sweet dancing doll that must send me your love
floating in the air as a seedling would and land on my limb...
In the space that I've reserved for your bloom,
You need not keep on wailing.
Just follow your heart and land on my side.
And don't delay
O, Dancing Lady...
hear my plea tonight.

Bouquet of Words

Perhaps you might ask yourself
What goal is it of mine
To seek you not in person
But to write continuously
Of love, of devotion

These words are my flowers to you
Receive them in lieu of material things
For, though people say that nothing lasts forever
Ideas have a tendency to infect,
To inspire, to inject a like-minded being

And once a carrier of that inspirational bug
He or she goes forth and spreads the message of love
Stretching my thoughts of you to the ends of time,
A place only reached by God Himself

So upon receiving my flowers
Please take care to water my tree
Sit and ponder under its shade
And let it breathe your sweet exhalations

Feed that tree upon your endless prairie
And if you are so pleased
Give me the sign of your admiration
A mere word will fill me and quench my thirst

All I need is a glimpse of your art
That masterpiece hidden deep in your heart
For it is there that my passion dwells
For it is there that my love for you wells

Such is the passion between me and you
Like a river that flows in search of its muse
A conduit flowing across the dimensions
Collecting the waters of my inspiration

Three:

Love, too,

Flows Through Fingers Like Water

Love in Rigor Mortis

And when I arrived home
From that long night of waiting for your breath
Like a flower awaits the morning dew
I recognized myself no more, for something had changed.

In the mirror a face returned my gaze but it was the look of an older man
Because in the long night the minutes had transformed to years
And I was a kid in love no more.

Because when you left your lips had failed to allow
That you would return
And I feared for the first time
In the realization that you had never truly gone
Because you had never truly arrived and I was always alone.

And this truth struck me at the essence of my self
And the long night broke apart in the presence of daylight
Like a tinted window shattered by the truth of a bullet
                                        And I was able to see
But my eyes all they wished for was an eternal blink
And then to awaken behind the stars where all night long I had
searched for you.

Love in Rigor Mortis II—the Revisit

O, how I consumed hours of that emptiness
Wishing on a faint glimmering constellation
That what had passed was real
And that not only I had burned in fervent wanton lust—love?

But in the morning all was clear
And this old fool in ashes now of a passion gone by
Captured the memories with perfect vision
And realized that I had been the fire on my burning bed
And you the log that lay there to be consumed
For you did not consume but for the innocence with which I
singed your skin

So now shadows of the eve appear
And all that touches me is the wind that blows...
                              Whistling over and over
There is something to be gained in love lost

That my poem will once again foster a heart to feel
What my heart sought in the long night of your wake
When I proposed to bring back your heart from death
And found in you that hollow grave where I entered thrice
And there would stay never to be seen again

Winter Love

The nights don't last
Its 6 am
Love is on the rocks
A fleeting moment
Inhale
then
hold your breath
as long as you can
until your lungs burn
Then you know you loved
Then you exhale
Then your love is dead

Nothing ever lasts
The strange car is running
down the road with no headlights
The night has died
under the oak tree
in the yard

Daylight begins to lift
the night's corpse
A strange dog runs
down the street
with no headlights
He's going the wrong way
Where is the watcher
To make the wrong things right?

When love died last night
a thief robbed me
She robbed my trusting heart
She wore me endless nights
Its 6 am
Its wintertime

Soul's Budding

My hand twitches as I type.
I don't know what it could be.
Perhaps the passing of a soul from this plane to the next?
Perhaps the thought that life is going, going, and I have made mistakes.
Will I get to redeem them before I go too?
Index finger cowardly shifts away from the F key, the starting point.
What could it be? A realization? We are alone.
No matter how many seeds we plant, the soul is solitary.
No matter how many kisses grow roots through our skin
they can never touch the inner light.
Only whisper to it a promise that cannot be kept.
"I will always be there for you..."
And then the end.
A journey that has no guide.
An ear that hears nothing.
A memory that's washed away.
A bouquet of affections rotting by the wayside...of that lonely road.

STD Romance

When you came the first time
You left me dripping
Like a faulty faucet
I said its okay
because it's love
We clapped together
in the euphoria of
new beginnings
We were high on life
and mostly weed
I talked about a wedding
You hid behind the clouds
O, Little bird flying so high
Won't you ride my face tonight?
It was lucky I didn't break out in my throat
But we broke through
that spell
Of that drip drop
Lick my cock
Cherry pop
And we common lawed
Yet I saw that hawk
Standing in the tree outside our window
Looking at the fruits I picked
But no 'mount of hissing and shooing worked cuz you held that
thinly knit string-a-ling
And just before you were depart
Alas! A tingling on my parts
So I thought O coincidence
You close the door
the way you came
With this cyclical ending
You leave me to gawk
A drip-drop
Tick-tock
Jingle pop
On my cock

El Ave de Mi Inspiración

¿Dónde estará el ave de mi inspiración?
Ya no brilla el sol
Ya no me nutren las palabras
Ya no sonríe mi corazón
Ni caen los romances sobre mi cabeza
Mis oídos sufren la ausencia de su voz enternecida
En mi hay un abismo interminable
En él se pierden los sentimientos del ayer
Aquellos trocitos celestiales que surgían de su mirar
Y ahora mis ojos solo fuente de sollozos son
Solo soy en esta soledad inspirada de mí en mi sufrir
Se regocija porque me tiene atado al muro del dolor
Solo voy buscando recobrar
Las gratas sonrisas en plenitud
¿Cómo volver el tiempo atrás?
¿Cómo ser esos seres de luz y amor de nuevo?
Vana es la causa de resucitar el idilio ya perdido
Me voy por el camino del recuerdo buscando renacer

My Inspiration (Translation of *El Ave de Mi Inspiración*)

Where has my inspiration gone?
The sun no longer shines for me
The words which gave life are now dead
Cold and buried as my heart
And from above only rain falls
My senses miss her full effect
Only emptiness resides in me
A black hole where yesterday got lost
That glimmer of hope that emanated from her eyes
For which mine cry torrents of tears
I am alone, inspired now only by my grief
Inspired like a sadomasochist inflicting and feeling the pain
Looking perhaps to find yesterday's promise fulfilled
To recover that which made my heart sing
How to turn back time?
Will we be those beings of light again?
In vain I fight against a fate that cannot be changed
Perhaps my only chance is death and then rebirth

Love is a Fiesta in the Night

Fiestas 'till the sun comes up are gone
Me and you together in days and long nights are gone
Gone like the inspirations of love once lived
Gone are the days of our innocence

We were supposed to have been like newly born babes
In arms which held each other warmly
And now they only feel the cold reality
Of your absence that I dread

With the knowledge that one day – no doubt –
Arms will hold you again but they won't be mine
My arms now feel only a cold chill
Rising from my hands that now hold –
Not your face or the warmth of your skin –
But the cold sweat of a beer bottle that speaks to me
Of the days that have gone away

Like fiestas that now end at 3 a.m. leaving something to be de-
sired
Desiring the soft gaze of your eyes upon me…
Desiring the warm rays of a July sun in early rising
To find me grasping at cold beer bottles but neither meets me

Perhaps it is my age that I cannot drink 'till sun-up
Perhaps it is that I was changed when you were gone
For now only nights find me thinking of you
With the moonlight intoxicating in your absence

I loathe the arrival of the next sun's rays
That will shine on my loneliness
As yet another day goes on by
and I am still without you

Nothing consoles me, not even
Drawn-out fiestas which once brought joy
So I retire to my dark room to think of you again
As the fiestas of this life come and go
But you come to me nevermore…

Love on the Night Train

Ears hear music where disturbing sounds break the silence
At night, in a dreamy state, I talk to you
We drift together as smoke in the dead calm
And in the silence that ensues
When the conversation stills
I hear the music of the train outside your window
And though I am blind through the window of your phone
I picture you in your white robe
Your silhouette softly pushing the edges of your dress
You lie on your bed to sleep
You lift and I watch the train rustling the leaves of your tree
Pulling on the strings of my heart
It shrieks for you to wake up
Our love is passing us by
As you lay there weaving your dreams....

24 Hours

24 hours is a dream
a mere blink of an eye
sleep escapes me in your absence
Since you took away my nights

In these chambers a silence resounds
Pounding the walls of my head
All is fire, all is breath
All is arbitration caught up in lies

In midnight waking and four a.m. middays
Insomnia is my only companion
My mother says my brain will one day dry up
Like a raisin in the sun

All these waking hours dreaming
Of the moments in your arms yet hoping
I never find you, for when I find your arms
I find the cross that marks my grave

4:49 evening approaches
Tequila sits in its crystal splendor
Sauza Blanco... does she tempt me?
Does she know of my yearning for you?

Does she know my future?
To sleep is to dream, is it not?
So to dream is to be awake

Forgetting that hours
and minutes
and seconds
without you exist...and simply exist.

The elixir awaits to coat my broken heart
To lightly place me in soft pillows of heavenly clouds
Drowning in rivers of Sauza and lime juice and you on my mind
I lay down to dream...

Mi Amante Soledad

Se llama soledad
Es tan bella y a la vez...
Tan puta que a todos se entrega
Estoy seguro de no ser el primero en comentarlo
Aunque a su modo me siga siendo fiel

Pero es que la conozco tan intimamente
Que creo jamas haber vivido sin ella presente
Porque no me ha abandonado
Siempre anda rondando mis pasos
Aun viendo a otra en mis brazos

Me espera pacientemente
Sonriente como si guardara un secreto cual no puedo saber
Porque solo ella esta en liga con dioses del porvenir
Porque ha hechado las cartas de mi suerte...

Ha leido las lineas de mis manos temblorinas
Ha estado en la vispera de mis amaneceres
Al pie de las ventanas de mi alma asomandose en la profundidad
De un abismo solitario donde existo en su sofocante abrazo quiza
por siempre

Insiste en recostarse en mi pecho
Siento su frio aliento sobre mi piel
Como quien se revuelca
Entre pastos primaverales con la muerte misma

Y me hace el amor
Recorriendo sus dedos sobre mi cerebro
Despertando pasiones ya extinguidas
Aunque jamas hechadas al olvido

Soledad es mi compañera
Pero no la merezco
Porque aun entre la entrega
De su desenfrenada pasion

Mi corazon sigue en busca
De una nueva ilusion
Alguien quien me ayude a olvidar
El desquiciante amorio
De mi amante soledad…

My Lover Solitude (Translation of *Mi Amante Soledad*)

Her name is Solitude
She is beautiful and at the same time
A whore that shares herself with everyone
I'm sure I'm not the first to note it
Though in a way she is still faithful to me

But I know her so intimately
That I don't think I've ever lived without her
Because she›s never left me
She's always been there following my footsteps
Even when accompanied by another lover in my arms

She waits for me patiently
Smiling as if hiding a secret which I cannot decipher
For she is in league with the gods of fate
And has read my luck in tarot cards

She's read the lines upon my palms
And has been next to me in nights before my waking
At the foot of the windows to my soul peering into the depths
Of an abysmal loneliness where I exist in her suffocating embrace
perhaps for ever

She insists on lying upon my chest
Exhaling her cold breath on my skin
As one would feel
When rolling around on a prairie embraced by death herself

And she makes love to me
Running her fingers through my brain
Awakening passions which seemed extinguished
Though never gone extinct

Solitude is my companion
But I do not deserve her
For even in her passionate love strokes
My heart continues to seek
The promise of new love
Someone who'll help me forget
The disorienting fervor
Of my lover, Solitude

After All

After all this time
their hearts swelled inside
giving the sense of permanence to feelings
now on the verge of a final goodbye

What happens to hearts that burst
engorged of themselves in reveries of the mind
fictionalized by hope
cemented by touch that burns
the imprints of a lover's fingers

Lips that once shone with desire
shut tight now by fears greater than love
the flush of cheeks in the throes of tangled
tethering of bodies in synchrony now obscure

This day marks the death of innocence
where will their love go to extinguish
emptiness fills the vacant chambers in their chests
where once hope crafted smiles
with the raw materials of their wishful thinking

But after all they still have breath
see them limping across the scene
they have not fallen yet completely
waiting for the dust to clear

To be reborn again
with sun rays drying their tears
to recover some day
their busted hearts piece by piece

Four:

Fluidity of Identity

Change

Change is...
A mystery.
A challenge.
Red hot coals that keep your feet
moving, jumping, trying to walk through the pit
to get to cool ground on the other side.
Be careful when you get there.
When you are there, look for another pit.
Because the coolness of dirt invites complacency.
Just like the predictability of a stable and static arrangement
brings about lack of creativity and death.
Keep evolving even after evolving.
Never sit down to say, "I have arrived".
Only death brings the end,
and it does so only here on Earth,
for we know not the transformation on the other side.
I have been changing drastically for some time.
But all acceleration wanes.
Eventually a consistent rhythm
takes its place.
While this speed lasts,
it's surprising when memories catch my attention.
Then I remember that I was a different man.
Only weeks ago I was sprouting from the ground.
How far these leaves have come
awaiting fruits that already nurture emptiness.
My chest fills its void with dreams
while my mind creates and ignores it's longings.
There is no stopping now.
Clouds will part to make way.
The moon extends its hand.
The sun looks wary.
Icarus I am not.
My roots reach deep upon the land.
I cannot fall,
lest I be axed down by fear or envy.

Palabras del Río

Hay palabras nacidas en el río
Entre torrentes que fluyen por veredas
Como venas de un ser
que busca encontrar una sola voz

Hay palabras que hacen el eco olvidado del pasado
Surgir de entre cascadas de donde grita y reclama
"No se olviden de mí!"
Retumbando la tierra

A veces, las palabras se convierten en seres
Son bajos de estatura
Son diferentes a nosotros
Viajan sobre un ser feroz
Cual a veces los devora y aún así siguen su culto

Estos seres tienen ojos que piden una pausa
Sus bocas son templos de cuales nada impuro surge
Solo el clamor de un ser refugiado en la incertidumbre
Y estos seres extienden sus manos pidiendo clemencia

Es la bestia la que sus vidas consumió
Escupiéndolas sobre el río que sus palabras retumbó en nuestros oídos
Y buscando renacer sobre esta tierra soñada se colocan las almas mojadas
a la margen de la vida y la muerte
Buscando ser amadas y no deportadas, abortadas como fetos indeseables

The Terms of the River (Translation for *Palabras del Río*)

There are terms born of the river
Amid torrents flowing down pathways
Like blood through veins
Of a being that seeks to speak

These terms allow yesteryears echoes
Surge from within the whirling cascades which clamor
"Do not forget me!"
In resounding splendor

These terms transform into beings
Short in stature
Strange creatures
Who travel amid a ferocious beast
That preys and devours them at times
And yet they persist to ride

These creatures have eyes which seek pause
Their mouths are temples of innocence
Crying for help as refugees
Their hands extended to be rescued
from the mouth of the beast

Their lives have been swallowed whole by monsters
Chewing them and spitting them upon our river as the terms we
see emerge
Seeking to be reborn upon the Promised Land, their souls poised
on a precipice between life and death
Pleading to us so that we, instead of deporting them and aborting
them like undesired fetuses,
Choose to love them

Lost

All my fire dims as the days go by.
Hour by hour, minute by minute,
I am removed from the idea that I was.
But we are all reduced from that which we thought we would be
to that which we are allowed to manifest.
We're left there upon the ground,
like pealed skins of fruits that perished long ago;
like the shed skin of snakes that once had feathers and fed upon
human hearts;
like the black, wasted carcass of a sun that died at the hands of
ignorant men,
seeking to find truth and worth in a world that offers no clues
but tentative testimonies of the essence of man.
Who am I?
I am the echo of an ancient howl discharged in rage,
the product of a clash of entities that never knew
the power in themselves to act—to act not. In the monotony of
present life
how can I bridge the gap to that distant past?
That glorious age when man and woman were carriers of the sub-
stance of life
for the pleasure of the gods,
for the continuity of the universe
for the perpetuation of humanity itself.
There is no truth out there beyond the scope of our human eyes
much more than there is in our hearts.
That thread was severed and gods died of thirst.
Therefore, there is no right way because the way for us
always opposes self-sacrifice.
We fall for that luring animalistic essence to survive as the fittest
and ensure that any kind of progress toward truth fails.
And it happens at the personal level extending through ripples
across the sea of people,
creating that which we have inherited:
a perpetual struggle just to rise to our feet and act like men, like
women…god-like
Who am I?

I speak of the scars that mark the spirit when it is stained by the blood of the innocent.

What single-celled organism,
what peaceful animal,
what inanimate object can I morph into
to escape the shame of my forefathers?
Nothing. No one can flee.
Yet some fight back against the urge to condone their sins.
To what end? Everyone is guilty of this.
Perhaps so that we keep reminders of those that have been stricken down
to always seek to recover what we have lost among the rubble of temples thrown asunder,
for destiny demands that we regain that which is only ours to determine:
identity, history, and self-determination bringing peace of the spirit in ourselves for a while,
and the perpetuation of the life of this world for eternity.

Chicano Por Siempre, Chicano for Life

Soy Chicano!
Soy de sangre Mexicano
Soy de costumbre Americano
Vivo en el Barrio all my life
Because the barrio is in the mind...
Aunque me aleje de ti you're in my heart
Mi gente, mi mente
I am the dual sense of being and non-being
Ni de aquí ni de ayá
Chicanos piss off everyone
El Americano hates that I'm a trouble-maker
El Mexicano hates that I make trouble
        Keep cool fool or they'll deport us all to Chiapas, cabron!
Oye, pos I've always liked to visit 'da Mayan ruins
        No chingues, no sabes lo que dices
Chale, you gotta rock 'da boat
Rattle the tree branches a little...
Or else how the hell do we get the fruit?!
        Pos chíngate a trabajar piscando, huevón!
        Pinche Chicano cholo!
Chale, pinche Malinche marica!
Soy Chicano one hundred percent!
Though you might not like me, te llevo en mi Corazón
Mexicano
Americano
I both reject you and accept you
Because of my cosmic awareness we can coexist
Only those that know their place die and are forgotten
Long live the peace so we can celebrate the war!
Viva la vida para que viva la muerte!
Aquí de este lado del río me río
because Estamos Undidos Mexicanos   and
Estamos Undidos Americanos   but
At least feliz
de ser cien porciento
                    Chicanos!

The Dead Chicano

Este Chicano
Man of letters...y guayaberas
Little hat sitting on his head
Cool little leaf fluttering in the wind
He reads poems to ears that hear
                        gas-pfffrrt! (puro pedo!)
Flatulence flowing from this man
From his mouth, fajita hole!
Dead Chicano
Dead! Chingado!
He's reading his own obituary
He's reading his sad soliloquy
Because he never knew
The tenderness of being loved
In this world he never fit
His heart too big, too cosmic
We are ants here, little brown man
Chíngate el mustache
Someone else is driving your car
But thanks for building it.
It's a nice car, for everyone else
                        ...But you

Dead Chicano Poet
Die now your ghost y cai-fine!
Your ashes sit in a jar
Propping up books
That talk about you

Chicano Renacido

El Chicano muerto revive a diario
Se disculpa con nadie
Se despide de todos
Dice adiós y luego canta una canción
Dice adiós pero se queda

Chicano de todos los tiempos
Que encara toda situación
Su cara se metamorfea
Es como las olas del mar
Viene y va, viene y va

Ahora su espuma es ligera y clara
Otras veces es espesa y revolcosa
En las aguas de su mar
Existen múltiples esencias
Conciencias vivas y extintas

Pero el espíritu de su cuerpo mojado es eterno
...Mojado,
Chicano nacido del vientre extranjero
Que lo empuja a este lado
Lado que lo recibe con dolor en sus manos

Chicano es el Indio que permanence
Chicano es el Inmigrante que siempre arriba
Chicano es el Pocho perdido a medio camino

Chicano es el sol mismo cual aunque no es de aquí
Sigue su labor en anonimato
Y tampoco se va
se despide

Chicano Reborn (Translation of *Chicano Renacido*)

The Dead Chicano is reborn daily
He excuses himself in front of no one
And says goodbye to everyone
He says "so long" then sings a song
He says "so long" but never leaves

Chicano of the ages
Who faces all situations
His face metamorphoses
He's like the waves of the ocean
Now coming now going, ebb and flow

Upon landfall today his foam is light and clear
Upon landing tomorrow will be frothy and murky
In the waters of his ocean
Lies a multiplicity of essences
Consciences living and some extinct
But the spirit in his wet body is eternal

Wet...back—flow of the Chicano born of foreign womb
Pushing him upon this realm where we exist
This realm which greets him
With pain in its hands as his gift

Chicano is the Indian who's remained
Chicano is the Immigrant streams that never cease
Chicano is the Pocho stuck in-between
Chicano is the sun itself

Though not from here, the sun
Grants his needed labor in near anonymity
And also never leaves
But always says goodbye

South Texas Reservation

Here we are
In this South Texas land
Surrounded at all sides
By government entities
Encroaching on this growth
Trying to stunt the arms
That seek to stretch the hand
That seeks to reach out and grab
Its piece of identity
Trying to stop the head that seeks to expand
A consciousness that sits not knowing
In this reservation of sorts
Confined-limited
Trying to stop the legs
That seek to push feet upon ground
To gain a traction and get moving
Out of this stage of stagnation
On the old question:
Who Am I?
South Texas reality is elusive
Clouded by reality TV or
Hours spent living out
The passions, joys and tribulations
Of beautiful people in telenovelas
Speaking perfect Spanish
Nothing resembling our broken usage
Of both English and Spanish
Married by the force of our habits
To form the union of
Tex-Mex
Pocho lingo
The only thing that government
Officials cannot stop
Because language infects even unsuspecting
Mainstreamers in their English monolingualism
Blurting out the craving for a "taco"
Even if it's an abomination from Taco Bell
Or in talking of Texas places and heroes
Goliad/Hidalgo – One and the same

In South Texas there exists a reservation

Of the mind
Of the flesh
Of culture and history
Of tradition and influence
Can it be contained?
Processed, purified for American consumption
Wringed through the rollers
Of Border Patrol checkpoints
On both the North and South sides
Though the North points to an American U.S.
And yes, South Texas is surprisingly
Part of U.S.A.
Filtered through by suspicious eyes in green
Uniforms asking, demanding for papers!
"U.S. citizens, folks?"
Police exceeding their right to stop me,
Search me, interrogate me,
Threaten me with detention,
Incarceration, deportation, expatriation,
                              Obliteration

If only I could dye...
My skin pale white
American? Yes sir!
De América Yo Soy!
Don't stop me, Mr. Green
I am White, see?
My name was Sánchez
But now it's Sheen
Fuck it! It worked for that guy.
I am your citizen
I am your man
Just touring this South Texas land
I'm writing a book, don't you see?
About reservations
They ought to name this one soon
Someone should stop pretending
And open their eyes
When you are walled in on all sides
You're either trying to keep others out...
Or you are the one being kept in.

Paradise on Earth

Give me all your tired
Marchers of the desert
Let them come and
Reap what we have sewn,
Vast fields of hope
For a better life
For a better world
Let them sit at our table
And partake of the feast
Of justice and democracy
Of equality and freedom
Let their bones in the desert floor
Not bleach in vain on that
Path to Paradise on Earth obstructed
Let the bodies of those left behind in sand pits
Be the seeds which will sprout forth from the ground
And turn the deserts of the Southwest into an oasis
Filled with an abundance of the American dream.
And let the children of the river in South Texas
Who have never known the heat of the Sonoran desert
Never know the coldness of a deserted mountaintop
Let them see the Promised Land beyond
Shining like a beacon of liberty to the world!
Let their innocence be not
Dealt the blow of our rejection
Lest we wish to silence forever
The voices of the world that pray to God
With hope in their minds
Chanting U.S.A. U.S.A. U.S.A.
With the pursuit of life, liberty, and happiness in their hearts.

Bio

Gabriel H. Sánchez is a writer and poet from South Texas. He has been published in scientific journals, in scholarly publications, several anthologies, and has served as a transcriptionist/ translator for a Rio Grande Valley newspaper. He is a graduate of the University of Texas-Pan American with a Master of Science in Rehabilitation Counseling. Alongside writing, Gabriel is also an actor, having played the role of President Lyndon Baines Johnson in the play titled Pat and Lyndon by Archer Crosely. He writes a blog titled "Cross Sections" on his company website, www.thervaingpress.com. Gabriel is also a freelance writer with his most recent articles published through Yahoo! Voices as a Yahoo! Contributor Network member. He also serves as the Director of Public Relations for the Coalition of New Chican@ Artists, a non-profit organization.